ALBÉNIZ

TANGO

Arranged for
Violin or Viola and Piano

by Watson Forbes

MUSIC DEPARTMENT

OXFORD
UNIVERSITY PRESS

TANGO

(from *España*, Op. 165, No. 2)

Arranged by
WATSON FORBES

I. ALBÉNIZ (1860-1909)

Tango

4

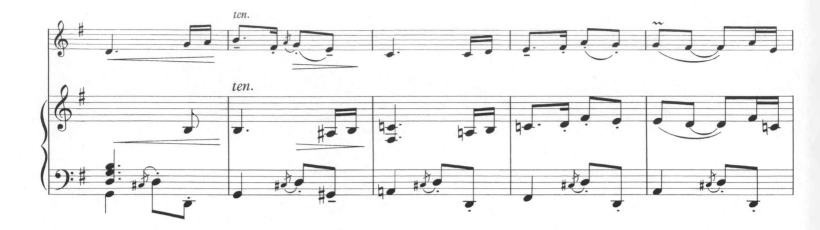

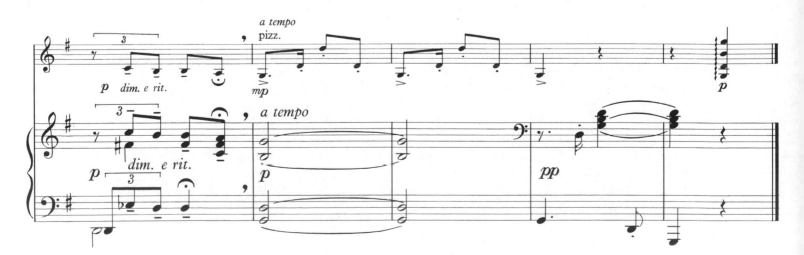

Tango

Processed and printed by
Halstan & Co. Ltd., Amersham, Bucks., England

OXFORD UNIVERSITY PRESS

Viola

TANGO

(from *España*, Op. 165, No. 2)

Arranged by
WATSON FORBES

I. ALBÉNIZ (1860-1909)

OXFORD
UNIVERSITY PRESS

www.oup.com

ISBN 0-19-355135-7

9 780193 551350